SPLIT MAP

Split Map

Rebecca Connors

Minerva Rising • Tampa
2019

© 2019 by Rebecca Connors

Cover Art: Landscape #20 by Liz Simmons
Instagram @misslizziepants

Published by
Minerva Rising Press
9501 Bessie Coleman Blvd #21802
Tampa, FL 33622-1082

ISBN: 978-0-9990254-9-9

www.minervarising.com

All rights reserved. Other than excerpts for review or commentaries, no part of this book may be reproduced without permission of the copyright holder.

To all those who get lost along the way,
& to Patrick and Olivia, who helped me find my way home

Contents

Judge's Notes	i
A Lifting Force	1
Aftershave	3
Anthem of the Elementary School Girls	4
The Intruder's Home	5
Climbing Magnolia	7
Firing Line	9
Spin the Bottle	10
Seven Minutes in Heaven	11
Ordinary Girl	12
Tim's on Acid and He's Driving	13
Corpus	15
Origin of Coordinates	16
To the Inspector	17
Out of the Chamber	19
Reelsville, Indiana, 1944	20
Imported	21
Split Map	22
Manual of the Vascular Flora of New England	24
Anything that Binds	25
How to Pack for the End Times	27
The Physics of Rebirth	28
These Ghosts Are Home	29
Acknowledgements	31

Judge's Notes

Reading Rebecca Connors's *Split Map* feels like slipping into a Southern afternoon. In the space between roses, cut grass, and magnolia breath, this subtle and powerful collection of poems invites the reader into the restlessness of home, the slippage of time, and the memory of places and histories fractured and re-formed into something more surprisingly intimate and beautiful. In "These Ghosts are Home," she writes:

… I'm the grasp
of never-finding. My ghosts

are my bedroom rug between
my toes, fox cries in our backyard
murmurs of my parents upstairs

in another world, one already
breaking…

No one speaks regret. My ghosts
smell like honeysuckle, a dusty
magnolia, a Sunday evening

thunderstorm. I am a knock
in the heart. A lost locket.

Connors's collection invites the question: in everyday life, in the lives of girls and women, what else can be revealed? *Split Map* invites the reader to look closer and to look again, to study the feeling between people, the passage of time, the displacement of spaces, and inhabit both the shock and delight of emptiness and moving on. In "Climbing Magnolia," she writes:

No tree will hold you, my mother
says, everything is fragile

up high. Birds, she says, are light enough
to balance branches.

& you are not a bird. But the tallest canopies
have a way of calling. Fragrant blossoms

& dusty black bark with knobs. I barefoot
& pull up to the first branch. I reach…
She is oblivious to my height. Maybe
I have lifted-off. In a moment, I will

full-circle the yard, swoop along
the honeysuckle, run my gingers

on the hot bricks on the side
of the house…

I am almost lost. Make my noise
as kin of this yard: damp grass,

slugs, crushed tomatoes. Like her,
my wings make no sound when I run.

In her poems, Connors explores how generations talk to one another, and how they observe, avoid, mark, or answer one another. Although several of the poems explore notions of inter-generational connection, disconnection, and mistranslation, Connors is not afraid to discuss issues of violence and trauma in poems such as "Urging," "The Intruder's Home," and "Origins of Coordinates." As a poet, Connors is not only aware of gender and power dynamics and the fallibility of her speaker and of characters on the page, but she is also keenly aware of the fallibility of the seemingly idyllic country world of Southern and Middle America. For example, in the poems "Out of the Chamber," and "Reelsville, Indiana, 1944," she explores how gun violence, religion, poverty, and the economic exploitation of farmers and farming communities have mapped and marked the American South and Midwest.

As a collection, *Split Map* is empowering and provocative in its response to both personal and social forms of violence. At the heart of this small but powerful collection of poems is the question: how can personal agency be formed and how, under even the most traumatic situations, can it blossom?

These are poems about female agency, about girls observing and partaking in the world, about women writing back, resisting, and remapping their narratives. In "Anthem of the Elementary School Girls," Connors writes:

> ... Catch us
> in a moment before fall, before science, twirling
> pencils, lips inclined to ears. At recess, we pass notes
> to boys, circle "yes" or "no." We learn pyramids,
> constellations and mummies. Imagine our sarcophagus –
> stickered notebooks, mix tapes, chapstick crammed
> into back pockets – testaments of our empire.

In this poem and throughout the collection, Connors notes how girls and women, in the process of their own identity-formation, can be both the object of the male gaze as well as the subject of their own the gaze (e.g. "At recess, we pass notes / to boys, circle 'yes' or 'no'"). Taking ownership of this dual role of playing both object and subject is further explored in poems such as "Firing Line," in which Connors writes:

> We just stand there, digging
> our heels into the carpet
>
> with our yellow barrettes
> and mom-picked party dresses
>
> at the edge
> of teasing and wanting, blushing up
>
> on the cusp of erupt.

Poems like "Firing Line" explore the vulnerability and power of women learning to define their roles in the world while still feeling uncertain of their current and future agency. And in this space of tenderness, of uncertainty, timidity, wonder and surprise, the speaker and women of Connors's collection learn how to respond to the male gaze, challenge complicity and decorum, subvert patriarchal and gender norms, and re-map their own worlds and futures.

Split Map is more than a collection of poems about coming-of-age, nostalgia, or childlike wonder, it is a journey through vulnerability into self-empowerment, and a story about how even in the most difficult of situations, female agency exists and reverberates, and how all women can dare to split maps, and thus, transform the world.

— Rita Banerjee, author of *Echo in Four Beats* and *CREDO*, and Director, MFA in Writing & Publishing, Vermont College of Fine Arts

Montpelier, VT | February 11, 2019

A Lifting Force

Stir your drink with a finger—ice clinks
and Scotch hangs with the heat.

Your solace: evenings on the deck
absorbing caramel stillness. Roses, cut grass,

your own sweat becomes a bouquet.
Your husband appears beside you,

narrating the sky as if you can't see
the violet clouds leaden. You wish

you still smoked. Dogwoods wave white fans
as your words slur to cotton. You've been waiting

for release—to will yourself into leaving
him. It would be like a bone-snap of thunder.

A flash. Leaves wallow, the wind swims
down, lifts hair from your neck. Another

crash. Closer to you. You raise your drink,
leave rings on the wooden railing.

One more thing for him to scold and
it's been 23 years and how many storms.

Your silence makes him sharp like an insult,
like raindrops flat smack against the deck.

You don't flinch. Green-grey rain douses the flush
of your skin. You know you're stuck. Inside, stagnant

with routine, he's forgotten you already.
Needing only convection, the storm moves on.

AFTERSHAVE

The beard fell in dollops
of shaving cream, a razor
removing thirty years

of growth, the nervous down-
strokes scraping an older
man, this startled stranger

with sudden cheeks balking
in the mirror. What else
would be revealed?

For what she saw
that afternoon, my father
never forgave my mother.

Anthem of the Elementary School Girls

After school, we leave doors unlocked. Bike twice
around the block unsupervised. Our skinned
knees escape our notice. Hair in knots,
whipping wind. I am all sprint and action. Hip-jut
balanced between poise and explosions.
Liz blasts the newest song and we sing sex
at full volume. We cut our hands on swing sets, dangle
our bodies from the top rail. Dare each other—

Pennydrops. Cartwheels. Our untucked shirts
billow over our upside-down heads. Catch us
in a moment before fall, before science, twirling
pencils, lips inclined to ears. At recess, we pass notes
to boys, circle "yes" or "no." We learn pyramids,
constellations and mummies. Imagine our sarcophagus—
stickered notebooks, mix tapes, ChapStick crammed
into back pockets—testaments to our empire.

Our parents grey a little more, call us to dinner
after hours pass, after street light shadows
among parked cars. We are the toughening up.
Bruised shins. Hearts dusted off.
We are the hand-knit sweaters cast off in fall,
bracing ourselves for the coming cold.

The Intruder's Home

It happens again. It always does.
Bourbon-drunk, he shouts your name.
You hope he'd forget. But then

your dad's hulking shape lurches
across the yard, a car released from its brake
growling through whispering men,

girdled women. A sea of spectators,
white-capped with gasps. Lock-kneed,
you wish refuge. He bellows insults

searing your face while you try
to comprehend what lit him. You know
he blames you for something

broken & your mom tries a salve
it's only a scratch – it's only –
but she knows you are enough

to make it worthless. Guests shift weight
until somewhere – laughter. A joke.
Your eyes dart to your father. He's still,

simmering. Someone turns the radio up.
Jazz flush. There's a new drink
in his hand. A smile irons his face.

What is the word for when the beast
turns away? It doesn't matter – you are
never not prey. The crowd absorbs him.

Wipe your palms against your Sunday dress.
You see stars in sunlight, the scuff
on your patent leather shoes.

This ringing in your ears. The afternoon
buffers the empty home in your chest.
Soon, the party is over & it happens.

He shouts your name –
even though he knows where you are,
even though he knows what heartbeats

flood the space between those words.
A cavern where you hold your breath
& shake & wait

his feet on the stairs to find you.

Climbing Magnolia

No tree will hold you, my mother
says, everything is fragile

up high. Birds, she says, are light enough
to balance branches.

& you are not a bird. But the tallest canopies
have a way of calling. Fragrant blossoms

& dusty black bark with knobs. I'm barefoot
& pull up to the first branch. I reach

hard-waxed leaves, arm past
pink-topped toothpicks of our crepe myrtle

& higher.
Cars passing by would never know

& higher.
Our silver shingles squint at me in

the summer heat. Somewhere below, my mother surveys
her rose bloom, beetles cling

to rusted fencing. The yard is full of rabbit-
eaten lettuces, deer droppings, ragweed.

She is oblivious to my height. Maybe
I have lifted off. In a moment, I will

full-circle the yard, swoop along
the honeysuckle, run my fingers

on the hot bricks on the side
of the house. Maybe she'll catch sight

of me—a flash of pink. Wonder how it came
to be so easy. Could I really leave her?

The tree-bones creak in answer. I scramble
my way down, trunk-smeared

bruises on my thighs. Emerging
from the forbidden boundary,

I am almost lost. Make my noise
as kin of this yard: damp grass,

slugs, crushed tomatoes. Like her,
my wings make no sound when I run.

FIRING LINE

We just stand there, digging
our heels into the carpet

with our yellow barrettes
and our mom-picked party dresses

at the edge
of teasing and wanting, blushing up

on the cusp of erupt.

SPIN THE BOTTLE

We sit in a circle
knees barely touching.
I am a nervous tug of hair.
My tummy in knots,
I hug my legs, willing myself
invisible. An empty Sprite bottle
lies in the center, dagger-ready.
This is a trap.
Dan tells us the rules—
but we know them already.
Even in sixth grade, we all know
who's a lucky spin. And even if he groans
in displeasure while his friends taunt,
he is eager. Sarah takes the first kiss.
A wiped mouth. The rough carpet
keeps sending the spin off course.
I count all my misses
like matchsticks
tamping down the flame

Seven Minutes in Heaven

The closet darkness must be
swimming underwater—
I can't breathe for what might be
happening among the coats.

We wait. Eyes locked on the doorknob.
Mark's antsy—it's been three
minutes and maybe his mom
will come in. We discover heaven
can be in linen closets, bathrooms, empty
pastel bedrooms—and here I am
in the den with Morgan
whose blond-white hair, crooked
teeth and rugby shirt make him
this heart-beating body.
The world is overbright and
we stare at each other's chins.
I think he's saying something
like make out to me
but blood hammers my ears too loud.
Will I say we did what? He comes
closer and my arms are cement.
I only want birthday cake,
bubblegum, the end of this party
in sight. Seven minutes is clenched
fists, blushes drained away. Forever
until the next game begins.

Ordinary Girl

Taller now, in her starched white dress,
she keeps phonograph cylinders, etched to render
all the words she might need to speak. Long-limbed,
she is a mast to what all the tall ships say
behind her back. Yet she doesn't blame the sea.

When she was five, she stood
transparent in the tall grass, her vowels
siphoned away by snakes. Taller now,
her mother convinces her that her face,
oval-beige, doesn't remind him of his first love,
only of what he cares to forget. Voices
like flies swirl around her head, conversations
at the table about her mute tongue, her empty
space. She cradles a jar in her chest filled
with pebbles, alphabet magnets, a broken
harmonica, pencil nub. She glows
when the world appears cherry-lipped
beside her with all the stories
she could ever want.

Hold still. Breathe.

We all have our own volumes, cadences.
This sepulcher of sound.

Tim's on Acid and He's Driving

I hear the senior girls
in the back seat I wonder how we made it
to the front, his thigh is right
next to mine maybe this speed is
for me I look to Rachel
she's beating time against
the passenger window
I am weightless floating
we careen streaks of light
as his beaten Buick unfolds ribbons
on MacArthur it's not even late but I
have already missed choir
I should have called my dad
no seat belts just my foot braced
below the dash cigarette smoke
and I don't know where to look
the world is coming at me
in blurred shapes I want to still
the girls in the back yelling
what the fuck you need
to slow the fuck down
he's already laughing
he's already hit the gravel
and when we lift off,
and begin to circle the axis
I blink calm like I knew
it would happen this way
my left arm around
Rachel my right behind
the seat my face
to her shoulder
an embrace
before impact
before shock before

pain before I knew
we shouldn't have been able to walk away.

Corpus

I am / my own architecture / keep your ears among my eaves / sometimes I whisper what dizziness, what destiny / when I'm feeling done with this solitude / my insides – wallpapered halls flooded with dust-mote breaths / I am / weight-bearing not up to code / here's the library: finger the worm-eaten plans, my wings admired but never constructed / catalog each tarnished lip / each bone strain / what light I let in shudders mice & moths / long-forgotten frailty & fur / turn this rusty joint in socket / here's the sore tooth / here's the broken turret / follow me to the root cellar, toes against raw-packed earth / crates of ghost-green potatoes, wheel spokes, a dried up gasoline can / my own lungs, own hips / tell the fat termites to eat this wood while I release concrete from its hold / condemn me / adjust to the crumble of a slated roof / of shingled mistakes / carry these spirals out of my spine / the egress & regrets full-stop—

Origin of Coordinates
for David

Map the monstrosities under our skin,
little brother, my holed-up hurt, my own
venom. How I left you curled up in your room,
the air snapping at our ears. Our parents sucking
every moment with their separation. Their smiles amplified
your hurt, your black T-shirt desolation. I had keys to the car
& so much depended on my exit. Will you let me be

the navigator now? I'll point out the landmarks
as we stumble along. The last dinner without arguing
or sneaking out to smoke or friends who knocked
on your window or your black sharpie-sketched worlds
or across the continent, establishing your own.
How I will someday walk back into that house
without a hello & this time take you with me.

To the Inspector

He never forgave me
for talking

measures my words
in quarts and
inverted lampshades—

I offer up so many

atlas and *magnolia*

forsythia and *sepulchre*

he wields a scalpel
for its thin angry neck

I say, *I love you all the way to 100*

he slivers words
into letters, shredded
vowels

endurance endure end

syllables discarded
half-eaten apples

regrets, my own hips, hum

I still believe
my words roll mountains

his negotiation, this nightmare

floating and flexing
against each other
a full bleed

my red words
blessing this exit

Out of the Chamber

Bullets in your soup, cracking teeth. Bullets littered
along interstates, swimming pools, shoulders. Bullets eating

all your air. Glossy and slim-coppered, bullets
skirting your legs in the office park. Stacking us

one by one, shelled, spent. Sparkling in playgrounds,
magpies making new games: catch as catch can.

Crimson-ended. Bullets teaching geography,
rattling like pins in the map. Here is this one

and then the next one and then another before
we can bury the last one. Here is a church choir

with notes punctuated by bullets. Here a parking lot,
a snowy afternoon, where there is space

between flakes for bullets. Here is your hand
in the popcorn finding bullets. Here is your last bouquet,

your knock-knock. Bullets finding homes nestled
in our chambered hearts, clinging to tissue

that will not forgive. At the gas station, bullets wait
to end where your life should be.

Reelsville, Indiana, 1944

This farm is a mixing bowl of dust, wilt stems
and manure. Corn tips wave in furrows, chickens

claw at baked dirt. The screen door slams, your boots
scrape against the cement. You raise your pipe

with callused hands. All you survey is mostly yours:
the cracked red barn, but not the bull. The fish

but not the pond. Two boys but not their fealty.
It's a penance: your back, your overalls

creased in oil. Your wife's making biscuits, her fingers
larded and sticky with dough. Bible readings

crackle on the radio. Evening peepers swell
as you're held in place. This vise grip of seasons

and scorn and Sundays. Everything comes again,
like sunrise, like eggs hatched to be killed, like you

sowing until the hereafter, neither above nor below
this Hell.

IMPORTED

Here, I am a *Yankee*.
Double-wides sag under Confederate
flags and the air feels blue despite
hard-baked heat. Here, my time

with him is a drive-thru.
He buys me Cokes and we idle.
Uptown shutters early, leaving
twilight to us. Soon enough,

he stops loving me, backing
away slowly as if he realized
I could never understand
the language. Churches line

the landscape damning me
on broken signboards.
I console myself with black tar roads
sunning snakes, all those red barns,

cotton silently screaming
in the fields. My eyes burn
in the sunlight filtered through
hickory trees blown green. I am

magnolia-kin. I jump to pull
a branch of blossom towards me,
inhale. We belong. Pull all the flower
into me. Stretch the scent

until I speak in tongues—
no one hears my *y'all's* or *bah's*
they fall from me like petals

Split Map

I'm driving your pickup
through the back roads

no idea where I'm going and you
are high, ranting grease fire

you turn to me, oxen dead
in your eyes, *am I dead*

I have to collar you
as you open

your door
to fly into blackness

I feel we're shucking off
it's just you and me and we

are alone together
you, hollow worms

me, still loving like the dirt
of the North Carolina roads I let

wander us home one hand
on the wheel the other

twisted into your red T-shirt
and we are both

screaming, I am so certain
you need me

I never slow down
the night sky

yawns over your pickup
summer bugs hum with the tires

there is nothing in the pines
or in the crosshatched stars

I expect the next morning
will bring you back

you rattle around the apartment
leaving me

the open door
saving you was not

enough I am gutsick
due North

Manual of the Vascular Flora of New England*

He hands me this John Lennon daisy. It stings
my insides like two-faced folklore. Cellophaned,
he feeds me saccharine nothings, claims my heart

is a tarantula, china-fragile. He wants to napkin-
wrap me, lift me over streams, candle my darkness.
How can he not know me? How a botanist

fingers raw earth, mapping sterile answers?
How I sleep with the *Iris petrana?* How I thrive
in muddy fields, spend my nights seeding sex-

tipped flowers? *Syringa vulgaris, Magnolia grandiflora*
consume my well-trained nose. One can't be
in the nursery forever. I give him the cold snap.

Say anthesis is over. Dead-headed—*celosia cristata,*
we're a felted cerebrum split between

---

* Title is from the subtitle of *Flora of the Northeast: A Manual of the Vascular Flora of New England and Adjacent New York,* 2007.

Anything that Binds

> . . . *he untied the green ribbon around his wife's neck. And her head fell off.*
> —The Green Ribbon, American Folktale

When I see my face strained in the mirror,
green ribbon garnishing my neck,

it would be an easy end. I almost have
the courage to do it. I keep this secret green

with me, because what would happen
if you knew? You would china-doll me,

guard my body hawk-like. Ribbon
long ago embedded in skin. I want

your hands everywhere but where they light
on my skin. I want your fingers along the crease

perfectly indenting my swallow. I can
be naked and still yoked. You can

be naked and still hope that one day
I may let my lips loose and tell you.

But I'm tied tight. I trace the veins
in your neck, pulse, rippling of shoulders,

my fastener for life. You married a slip,
one undone knot from death. Let's keep my lie

supported. Teach me how we must hold on
to this muscle connected

to sinew connected to bone
connected to the illusion

that nothing will ever break us.

How to Pack for the End Times

You don't—not really. It comes upon you
quickly. One moment at the grocery store
picking avocados, the next, smoke corsets
the skyline. We reach home—our daughter
wide-eyed as neighbors scurry along
in the red-wind. The emergency broadcast

system drones through cracks of the car-horned
city. This new reality seizes my throat.
What must it mean for us and for her?
How can I hold this together?
My body mechanical as we grab
phone chargers, coats, her blanket—
she follows me with her constant *why's*.

All I can do is keep moving. Busy my hands:
social security cards, ace bandages, a knife, juice boxes,
endurance, whatever medicine left on the dresser.
She offers up her pillow, demands to wear
her dress shoes. *Oh my heart.* Do I want to argue
in our list of last moments? As we emerge

into shattered streets, I want to cub
my family, pull their bodies into me. But
I can only cement my daughter's hand
to mine. Hold tighter than night
for the fleeing crowds want to surge
as tide and carry her away from me.

THE PHYSICS OF REBIRTH

The cracked red barn births a clutch
of baby chicks. And this is his chore,
to scoop and spread feed for scratching
and plucking. Scoop and spread. Bored,
maybe, he wrestles three chicks into his hand.
He's thinking of red capes and Superman's
phone booth, the comics of the big city,
as he walks to the bag of feed
to bury them. He urges the newly-
caved to use their appetite to escape. Perhaps
he believes they will. Then, he goes fishing.

The twilight comes and the others go on
clucking. The corn goes on willowing.
Tomorrow he'll watch the bull mount
whatever cow is ready. It will be
his mother, a few days later,
who uncovers the silent beaks,
the bony tufts of down.

These Ghosts Are Home

My family didn't intend it this way,
but we all left home, separately. My dad,
alone with all he'd rid himself of—

the house & everything in it.
What I couldn't bring with me, totems
of my teenage years, trashed.

Haunted by the inventory
of what's missing, I'm the grasp
of never-finding. My ghosts

are my bedroom rug between
my toes, fox cries in our backyard,
murmurs of my parents upstairs

in another world, one already
breaking. My brother will not
go back. Empty-footed, he knows

how little our childhood was kept
intact. I could not hold onto it all,
my dad let go of the rest.

No one speaks regret. My ghosts
smell like honeysuckle, a dusty
magnolia, a Sunday evening

thunderstorm. I am a knock
in the heart. A lost locket.
My diary left crammed

in the bed frame. I would sneak
outside, sit with lightning bugs
busy dotting my future. I'd smoke

cigarettes in the black-blue night,
dreaming of distance and return,
thinking I would never be uprooted.

Acknowledgements

I am grateful to the editors of the following magazines in which the following poems have first appeared, sometimes in earlier versions:

Bird's Thumb: "Tim's on Acid and He's Driving"

Dialogist: "Corpus" (as "Loculus"), "Out of the Chamber"

Menacing Hedge: "To the Inspector"

Tinderbox Poetry Journal: "The Physics of Rebirth," "Split Map"

I would also like to thank my teachers, past and present: Megan Fernandes, Christopher Hennessy, and especially Rebecca Morgan Frank and Jennifer Givhan for their mentorship in reviewing and helping me shape this book. Thanks to Rita Banerjee for selecting my manuscript and Emily Shearer at Minerva Rising Press for her careful edits. To Liz, for sharing your art. Thanks to my high school English teacher Dr. Galvin for instilling the love of poetry into me all those years ago. To the Bourbon Poets of Boston, your feedback and support cannot be matched. Hearts to my friends and family all across the map, especially Mom, Dad, and David. And lastly, love to my partner Patrick and my daughter Olivia, who make my days happen.

Author Biography

Photo by Patrick Connors

Rebecca Connors graduated from Boston University with a BA in English. After graduation, she spent time roaming across the map. Raised in Bethesda, MD, she has lived in the small town of Shelby, NC and on the west coast, in San Francisco, CA and Seattle, WA. She is now back in Boston with her family, where she is an MFA candidate at the Solstice Creative Writing Program at Pine Manor College. Along with her writing and studying, she uses her digital skills to enact change and volunteers at her daughter's public school. She has too many plants and a weakness for regency romances, murder stories, and disease ecology. She also has a tuxedo cat. Her poems can be found in Rogue Agent Journal, The Hunger Journal, Menacing Hedge, and Tinderbox Poetry Journal, among others, and have been nominated for the Pushcart Prize and the Orison Anthology. *Split Map* is her first chapbook. You can follow her on Twitter @aprilist or visit her site at aprilist.com.

www.ingramcontent.com/pod-product-compliance
Lightning Source LLC
Chambersburg PA
CBHW032005060426
42449CB00031B/728